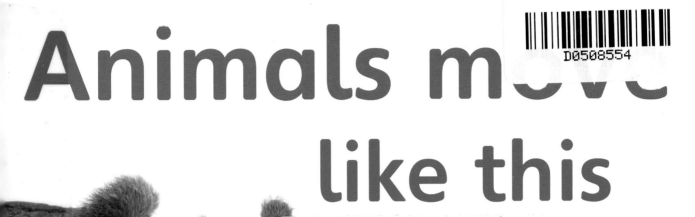

Animals move like this

Bobbie Kalman

 Crabtree Publishing Company

www.crabtreebooks.com

Created by Bobbie Kalman

Author and Editor-in-Chief
Bobbie Kalman

Educational consultants
Elaine Hurst
Joan King
Jennifer King

Notes for adults
Jennifer King

Editors
Kathy Middleton
Crystal Sikkens

Design
Bobbie Kalman
Katherine Berti

Print and production coordinator
Katherine Berti

Prepress technician
Katherine Berti

Photo research
Bobbie Kalman

Photographs by Shutterstock

Library and Archives Canada Cataloguing in Publication

Kalman, Bobbie, 1947-
    Animals move like this / Bobbie Kalman.

(My world)
Includes index.
Issued also in electronic format.
ISBN 978-0-7787-9564-3 (bound).--ISBN 978-0-7787-9589-6 (pbk.)

        1. Animal locomotion--Juvenile literature. I. Title. II. Series:
My world (St. Catharines, Ont.)

QP301.K335 2011   j573.7'9   C2010-907444-0

Library of Congress Cataloging-in-Publication Data

Kalman, Bobbie.
 Animals move like this / Bobbie Kalman.
     p. cm. -- (My world)
    Includes index.
  ISBN 978-0-7787-9589-6 (pbk. : alk. paper) -- ISBN 978-0-7787-9564-3
(reinforced library binding : alk. paper) -- ISBN 978-1-4271-9671-2
(electronic (pdf))
 1. Animal locomotion--Juvenile literature. I. Title.
  QP301.K278 2011
  573.7'9--dc22

                                            2010047639

Crabtree Publishing Company

www.crabtreebooks.com   1-800-387-7650

Printed in China/022011/RG20101116

Published in Canada
Crabtree Publishing
616 Welland Ave.
St. Catharines, Ontario
L2M 5V6

Published in the United States
Crabtree Publishing
PMB 59051
350 Fifth Avenue, 59th Floor
New York, New York 10118

Published in the United Kingdom
Crabtree Publishing
Maritime House
Basin Road North, Hove
BN41 1WR

Published in Australia
Crabtree Publishing
386 Mt. Alexander Rd.
Ascot Vale (Melbourne)
VIC 3032

What is in this book?

Why do animals move?

Most animals move.

They move to find food.

They move to keep safe.

Animals also move
to play and have fun.

Animals move in different ways
because their bodies are different.
Name five ways that the animals
on this page are moving.

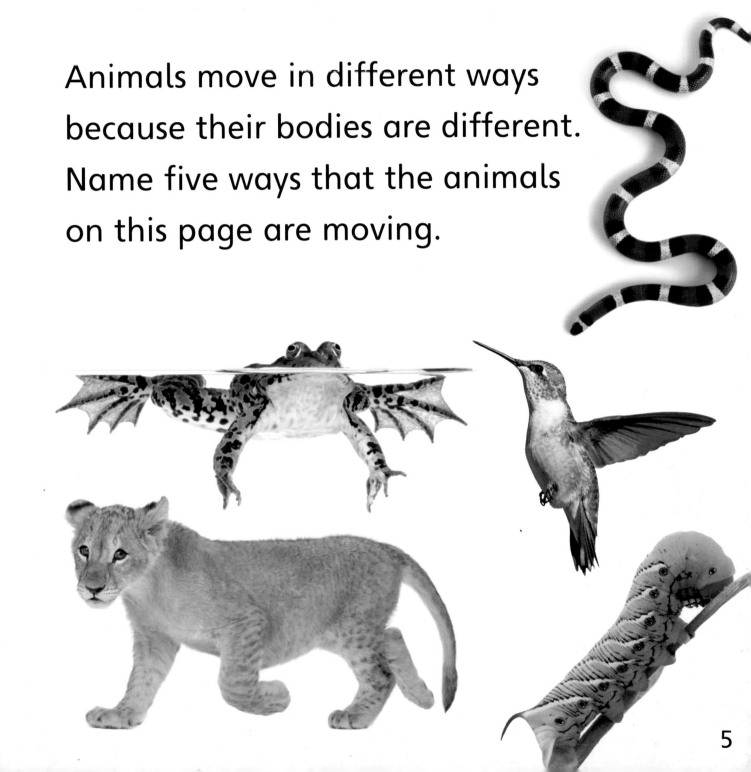

How many legs?

Some animals have two legs,
and some animals have four legs.
Animals with two or four legs
can walk and run.
Some can also swim
and climb.

chipmunk
walking

gibbon
running

Some animals have many legs.
Caterpillars, centipedes, and
millipedes have more than four legs.
They use their legs to crawl and climb.

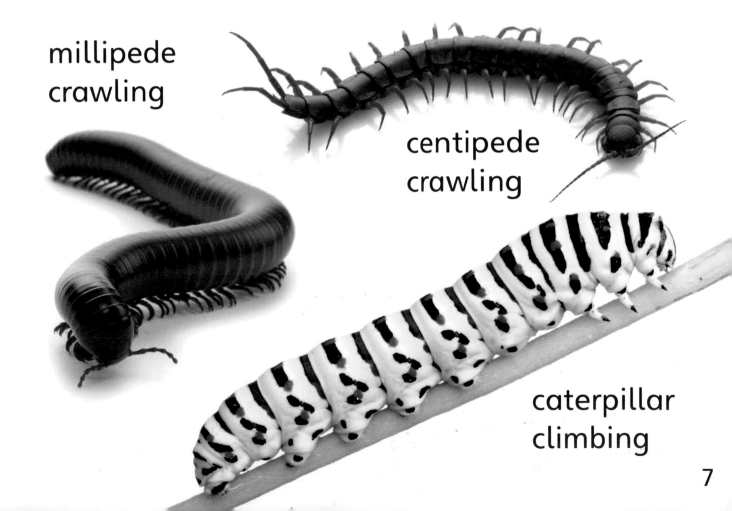

millipede
crawling

centipede
crawling

caterpillar
climbing

Up in the trees

Some animals spend
most of their time in trees.
They find food in the trees.
Their babies are safer
high up in the trees.

orangutan mother
and baby

branch

spider
monkey

Some animals have
long arms.
They use their arms to
swing from tree to tree.
Some animals have
long tails, too.
They use their tails to
hang on to branches.

Climbing high

Many animals live on **mountains**.

Some mountain animals have **hoofs**.

Hoofs are hard feet.

Hoofs keep animals
from slipping on the rocks.

hoof

mountain goats

rocks

mountains

bighorn
sheep

hoofs

11

Flying in the sky

Animals that fly have **wings**.

Most birds can fly.

Birds fly by **flapping**

flapping wings

their wings up and down.

Birds also **glide** when they fly.

They glide without moving

their wings very much.

gliding

Bats can also fly, but they cannot glide.
They have to keep flapping their wings.
Butterflies can fly.
They **flutter** by flapping their wings fast.
Butterflies can also glide
the way birds can.

gliding

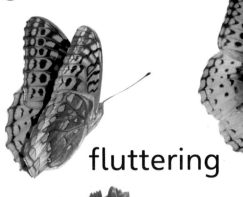

fluttering

Hop, leap, pounce

Rabbits **hop**, or make small jumps.

Frogs **leap**, or make big jumps.

Both rabbits and frogs have long, strong back legs.

The frog is leaping.

The rabbit is hopping.

Foxes **pounce** when they hunt.
To pounce is to jump quickly
and quietly on top of something.

The fox is pouncing on a mouse.

Slide and slither

Some animals do not have legs or arms.
They move by **sliding** from place to place.
A snail moves on one foot under its body.
Its body makes a slime called **mucus**.
The snail slides on the mucus.

A snail has
a shell.

foot

mucus

Snakes slide their bodies in **curves**.
Curves are lines that are bent.
Moving this way is called **slithering**.

curve

curve

curve

How do they swim?

Many animals live in water.

Their bodies are built for **swimming**.

Fish move their **fins** to swim.

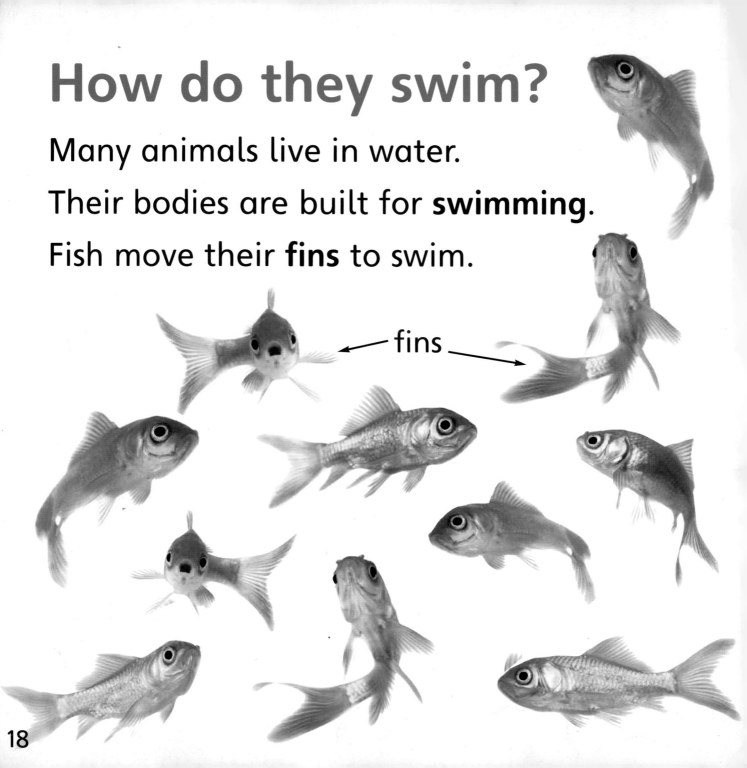

fins

Dolphins are not fish, but they live in water.

Instead of fins, dolphins have **flippers**.

They move them up and down when they swim.

Dolphins also leap high out of the water.

flipper⟶

Dance moves

Some animals look like they
are **dancing** when they move.
Which dancer do you like best?

Do you move like this?

Do you move the way these children are moving? Write down or draw all the ways you move in one day.

jump

ride

walk

dance

climb

pump

Words to know and Index

climbing
pages 6,
7, 10, 22

crawling page 7

dancing
pages 20–21, 22

 flying
pages 12–13

hopping
page 14

leaping
pages 14, 19

pouncing
page 15

running
page 6

sliding
pages
16–17

slithering
page 17

swimming
pages 6, 18–19

swinging
page 9

walking
pages 6, 22

Notes for adults

Objectives
- to help children identify how animals move
- to have children understand why animals move in different ways

Questions before reading
"Which body parts do we use to move?"
"How do animals move? What body parts do they use to move?"
Tell the children to look at the title page of the book before you read and ask them:
"What is the sloth doing?"
"How is it holding onto the branch?"
"What do you think it does in the tree?"
"Which other animals live in trees?"

Questions after reading the book
"Why do animals move?" (to find food, stay safe, play, and have fun)
"Which animals crawl?" (millipede, centipede, caterpillar)
"Which animal slithers?" (snake)
"Which animals slide?" (snail and snake)
"Which animals climb?"(monkeys, chipmunks, orangutans, mountain goats, caterpillars, bighorn sheep)
"Which animal swings?"(monkey)
"Which animal leaps?" (frog)
"Which animal pounces?" (fox)
"Which animals run?" (gibbon, lion, cheetah, horse, dog, and many more)

"How do fish move?" (They swim with fins.)
"How do dolphins move?" (using flippers)
"Which animals flap and flutter their wings?" (Birds and bats flap, and butterflies flutter to fly quickly.)

Activities: Dance attack!
Play animal sounds and let the children dance and move like the animals in the book. Stop the music and have them freeze in an animal motion.
Set up four different centers with pictures of trees, mountains, swamps, and oceans. Have children draw and label some animals that belong in each.

Animal parade
Have the children make masks of some animals from the book. Then parade around the school, using animal moves.

Extension:
How does it move?
Read Bobbie Kalman's book *How does it move?* to the children and expand their experience with animal, plant, and human moves.

Guided reading: J

For teacher's guide, go to www.crabtreebooks.com/teachersguides